Light Volumes
Dark Matters

Claudia Dutson

Light Volumes Dark Matters
© 2010 Helen Hamlyn Centre, Royal College of Art
ISBN 978-1-907342-24-0

British Library Cataloguing-in-Publication Data. A catalogue record for this book is available from the British Library. All rights reserved. No part of this publication may be reproduced, stored in a retrieval system or transmitted in any form or by any means, electronic, mechanical, photocopying, recording or otherwise, without the prior consent of the publishers.

Published by
Helen Hamlyn Centre
Royal College of Art
Kensington Gore
London SW7 2EU
+44 (0)20 7590 4242
hhc@rca.ac.uk
www.hhc.rca.ac.uk

Author **Claudia Dutson**
Editors **Jeremy Myerson and Rama Gheerawo**

Design **Ann-Kristina Simon**
Artworking **Household**

Printer **Beacon Press**

Cover Paper **Hello Silk 350gsm (FSC Mix Sources)**
Inner Paper **Munken Lynx 120gsm**

Cover Image **Frankfurt at night** © the Author

Preface **Sharon Pang**	7
Foreword **Jeremy Myerson**	9
Introduction	11
Light Volumes **Dark Matters**	17
Light Switch **Dark Adaptations**	39
Light Structures **Dark Infrastructure**	61
Bibliography	69
Index	71

Preface This publication is supported by the Megaman Charity Trust Fund, which was established in February 2008 to support programmes and projects specialising in education and environmental protection. Megaman is a leading designer, manufacturer and marketer of innovative lighting solutions and equipment. It is probably best known for its pioneering work on innovative designs of CFLs and LEDs that enable the replacement of less efficient light sources in a wide range of applications.

The research project on which Light Volumes, Dark Matters is based, is the first undertaken by Megaman Charity Trust Fund in partnership with the Helen Hamlyn Centre at the Royal College of Art, London. It addresses an issue of vital importance. It effectively challenges current practice in lighting design, enshrined in UK lighting codes, that is based on inflexible engineering measures of productivity rather than a practical and imaginative response to people's real needs.

I have been impressed with the creativity and diligence of researcher Claudia Dutson in investigating the current state of lighting for the workplace environment and coming up with fresh thinking that sets out an alternative vision based on more inclusive and energy-efficient values. We are very likely to continue our research cooperation with the RCA in the future. Claudia's expertise and enthusiasm has resulted in a body of work that makes a valuable contribution to knowledge in the lighting field. I hope this book will give insights to architects, lighting designers and specifiers and draw more people's attention to people-centred, sustainable lighting design.

Sharon Pang, Megaman Charity Trust Fund

Foreword If you have ever sat for hours under a fluorescent strip in a uniformly bright office far from natural light, or worked in a retail showroom uncomfortably hot with a thousand lamps focused on the merchandise, you will recognise the lighting conditions that Claudia Dutson describes so eloquently in this publication. It has become an inescapable fact that many of our commercial interiors—shops, showrooms and offices—are over-illuminated. This is an unsustainable approach for the environment and detrimental to the wellbeing of workers.

Light Volumes, Dark Matters tackles current lighting practice head on. The art of lighting is presented here in all of its facets—physical, psychological, architectural, biological and cultural—and the author never shies away from the complexities and inherent contradictions of the subject matter. The study of the language of light and dark is an especially novel approach in a research project that has ranged far and wide over the field, consulting experts, conducting light experiments and collaborating with users.

The Helen Hamlyn Centre, which was established at the RCA in 1999 to provide a dedicated research focus for people-centred design, has long wanted to address lighting design, as technology moves much faster than human biology and perception. In its tone and form, the book consciously recalls the short, iconic treatise on aesthetics, In Praise of Shadows, by the Japanese novelist and author Junichiro Tanizaki, which is revered by many architects. We hope that Light Volumes Dark Matters raises the consciousness of designers in the same way.

Jeremy Myerson, Helen Hamlyn Centre, Royal College of Art

Introduction This book is the outcome of a two-year project carried out at the Royal College of Art Helen Hamlyn Centre and supported by the Megaman Charity Trust Fund. The project set out to investigate why levels of artificial light in commercial interiors are increasing and explore more efficient ways of lighting space than with a uniform lighting layout. The primary concern of the research was the impact that high levels of light have on the people who work under them.

Artificial lighting is one of a set of conditions in the built environment that has been identified as having a profound effect on a person's physiological and psychological health. Light does more than enable vision. It is important to approach lighting design from this position since the inclusion of such information in codes for lighting is contingent on establishing, at the outset of a lighting scheme, the correct level of light for visual tasks. Once that level is set there is very little room for manoeuvre to go on to address the more subtle and variable perceptual elements of lighting.

Traditionally the conditions for interior lighting have been derived from a mechanical interpretation of productivity. This is the amount of light needed to complete a visual task. In an office, the idea of productivity is directly linked to the brightness of light; the more light, the faster a task can be completed with accuracy. In retail, the lighting is based on a psychology of sales, the eye being attracted to the brightest points in a visual field. Both of these often result in over-lit and unstimulating environments in which to work. The qualities of light that can support other needs of employees are largely absent. Furthermore, an excessive level of artificial light in offices and commercial interiors puts stress not just on those who work there, but also on the environment through high levels of energy consumption.

The research has reviewed two trends in architectural lighting: a sustainable approach where the amount of light is reduced through technological interventions, such as automated switches and low-energy solutions; and a wellbeing approach where levels are raised to stimulate alertness. The limits of these approaches initially suggest that as long as there is a certain quantity of light in a room, it will have a desired and predictable outcome, regardless of how this is achieved.

The research project that this book draws on occupied a space between these conflicting strategies, by considering light as a qualitative rather than quantitative entity, to suggest alternative methods for approaching architectural lighting. The research explored cultural and physiological perceptions of light; variables such as hue, colour, direction and movement; the physical and temporal properties of light with particular reference to the person who is experiencing it; and the technology of lighting.

The nature of this book is to critically reflect on the application of artificial light in buildings. It is not a new set of rules or guidelines but instead intends to challenge the existing paradigm of codes and standards for architectural lighting. It asks designers and architects to rethink the way they execute lighting in a workplace and give space for the serious consideration of the subjective impressions of those who will be using the light.

The book is structured around two main essays. The first chapter, *Light Volumes Dark Matters*, breaks away from the paradigm of seeing light on surfaces and is a critique on the flatness of light, both as a method and an end result. Viewed instead through the architect's eye and the eye-like anatomy of windows, the chapter reveals the stark difference between our experience of natural light and artificial light. The phenomena of extreme light environments—pure colour light installations and semi-darkness—are explored through the physiology of the human eye. The importance of darkness is shown to be more than merely an absence of light.

The second chapter, *Light Switch Dark Adaptations*, investigates the technology of delivering and controlling light, and its effect on the body. Lighting controls are interrogated in order to understand the real problems with sustainable lighting that architects and designers need to address. The chapter also challenges current ideas about the biological and physiological effects of light.

The conclusion, *Light Structures Dark Infrastructures*, continues the analogies of evolution and adaptation into the concept of legacy by setting the problems outlined in the book against the context of speed and time.

Throughout the book a series of observations, working practices and encounters with people who have provided valuable insights are documented. The cultural perception of light is illustrated through diagramming the language used to talk about light. A travel diary forms an account of the two main threads of thought that occupy the research. The index at the end of the book expands on concepts explored in each chapter and is referenced in the main body of text.

I have had two years to think about light. It is not nearly enough time to address everything that has come to my attention. In addressing the very first question set by the research brief, the full scale of a project dealing with light was revealed. Light, I discovered quickly, is about everything; science, philosophy, language, art, natural history, culture, theology. With this in mind, I hope in eighty pages to give enough space to the subject to sketch out a field for rethinking light, particularly for those who are not scientists, engineers or lighting experts.

Light Volumes
Dark Matters

Light Volumes Light, in the architect's eye, is the animating substance of architecture—with it, the building comes alive. Light is attributed with having a special quality that almost consecrates the architect's building. Le Corbusier's definition of architecture as being the *masterly, correct, and magnificent play of masses brought together in light* suggests that architecture cannot exist without light; without it there is nothing to see, leaving the perception of space to touch or hearing.

While architectural monographs on Le Corbusier, Louis Kahn or Alvar Aalto provide numerous quotes about natural light and architecture, most architects have little or nothing to say about artificial light. It has been left to writers and thinkers of the early twentieth-century to fret about the abundance of electrical illumination and its philosophical implications, and more recently, engineers and designers to worry about its environmental ones.

The architect's treatment of artificial light is curious. It is a separate animal from natural light, consigned mostly to the ceiling as if—like a child's rudimentary depiction of the sky—light only comes from above. The techniques of lighting a building might be described as being either functional, sculptural or advertorial. The colour-changing light thrown on façades and on lobby walls references, not the dynamism of light in nature, but the flicker of a television screen or the changes that sweep across a mechanical billboard.

Artificial light does not animate architecture in the same way as natural light. But architecture is instrumental in animating light. Light doesn't simply travel from a source—the sun or a light-bulb—onto the surface of an object and into the eye. It bounces, refracts and scatters off the materials it comes into contact with, its properties altered at a micro-scale as wavelengths are selectively absorbed or reflected by pigments in the material. In a room, the changing qualities of natural light over the course of a day are mediated through the architectural form; orientation of the window openings and the room interior.

To illustrate this point, one could consider windows as architectural *eyes*, whose outer elements (frame); those at the threshold (glazing) and the cavity (room) are a complex arrangement that modulate light. In re-examining a decorative window detail, typical to the Regency architecture in much of central London, this opening can be seen to be more than a plane of luminance on the wall.

The Georgian window takes up almost the entire floor-to-ceiling height in order to maximise the amount of light reaching the far end of the room. Around its outside edges are decorative mouldings; a brow above—in the form of a pediment, cornice or lintel—protects the upper half of the window from direct sun at midday, while the painted sill reflects light into the room. As the building cannot move over the course of the day to avoid sunlight, the windows have a moulded architrave or pilasters at each side, performing the same function at times of the day when the sun is low in the sky. Only a small protrusion is needed to create long shadows in the morning and evening. The ornamental elements are not explicitly engineered to perform as shading devices and it might be fair to consider them a decorative conceit. Nonetheless the accumulative result of these elements *thicken up* the window. It becomes a three-dimensional volume where the light constantly changes with the shifting arrangement of volumes, in relation to each other and the path of light.

Inside the window are a series of *eye-lids* that can be closed fully or partially to reduce the amount of light that enters. Wooden shutters, often painted white, can be folded back into the deep window surround, where they double as another semi-reflective surface to gather light and bounce it into the room. Further layers of curtains, voiles and blinds can be added to bring down the intensity of light.

The anatomy of a skylight—a peculiar thing that looks

upwards rather than forwards—describes a simple light-collecting eye that has no use for capturing images or views. Its deep socket, usually painted white, gathers light efficiently without bringing too much glare into the room as the sun is only momentarily perpendicular to both top and bottom openings.

The modernist window is a high-definition wide-angle vision machine. Optimised for gaining a panoramic view, it is quite independent of the building's structure—not restricted in size by the structural loads that have to be carried vertically through the wall. This window is equipped with louvres, visors, blinds and optical-coatings; technical accessories to deal with the environmental side-effects that come with the uninterrupted view—solar gain and glare.

As the thickness of architectural form has been succeeded by modernist ideas of lightweight construction and functional detailing—ceiling decorations have been removed; architraves around windows pulled tight; pediments, cornices, and any other unnecessary fattening up of the architectural fabric flattened out—architecture deals with light in a mechanical way. Wrinkle-free buildings freed from historical ornamentation present picture-perfect architecture. The straight edges, flush glazing details and even planes of the modern style create not only a new architectural language but a distinctly direct language of light. Variables are excluded as the light that was once subtly manipulated through the architecture and modified using shutters, curtains or screens comes straight in through the window.

The planning of light in architecture ensures a flatly uniform level of light upon a flat horizontal surface. The convention of the reflected ceiling plan allows little chance to explore the qualities of light and its volumetric potential. It is a literal expression of an infrastructure of delivering light that favours the geometry of the circuit diagram (rectilinear and even) over that

inherent in light (conical and gradated). Furthermore, it is focused on what lies directly beneath the luminaire on another flat surface—the notional working plane, 0.7 metres from the floor. The exercise of light planning is concentrated on achieving a numeric value at this datum and in providing uniformity throughout the room.

The future promises ever flatter self-illuminated technology. It is the drive behind technical progress; each latest innovation presenting an ever finer sliver of technology capable of doing what could once only be achieved with bulky machinery. Consequently, the flatter these objects, the *lighter* they become. These flatland dreams are occupied by an idea of light altogether different from that provided by incandescent or candle light. A concept of *lightness*—in the sense of a lack of heaviness as well as a luminosity—is particular to this dream. Light has tried to free itself from the associations that weighed it down; its shadowy past eradicated through diffusion lenses and filters; its burden of heat separated from it through fluorescent and LED technology.

The convergence of television and computer display technology with lighting means that our work illuminates itself, apparently dispensing with the need for a reading lamp. The words also take on a lightness; no longer situated on the surface of a page in a book, they levitate in the ether of virtual memory, recalled when needed, to appear on the computer screen.

Stemming from religious ideas of enlightenment being accompanied by light, the strong cultural association of the transmission of light being the transmission of information remains. The objective, singular truth of religious epiphany, communicated through direct light streaming from the heavens, has given way to the possibility of a multitude of truths and democratisation of information sources delivered through the unidirectional, diffused light of the self-illuminated flat screen.

Flat, diffused light is without volume or structure and has neither spatial nor temporal consequence. As we look through the window of the computer screen, we no longer expect the light that streams from it to be of the time and space that we occupy at the present.

———

The way that we see is more complex than we realise. Typically we might imagine our own vision to be something like a cinema screen, a flat surface onto which a picture of the world is projected to be *seen* in our brain. But sight is a peculiar sense in that we do not see directly. The back-to-front, upside-down images received on the retina are not corrected by optical apparatus, but sent as signals to the brain. This is not visual information sent in the form of a real picture, but information about luminosity and colour that the brain constructs into a virtual image.

We have become used to seeing light only where it comes into contact with a surface and so our relation to light has been for the most part a story about passive visual perception. But optical phenomena of light—a rainbow, or the saturated light installations of artists Carlos Cruz-Diez and James Turrell—show that light and the eye have an important spatial and geometric relation. These phenomena are products of refraction, one happening in space as varying sizes of water droplets refract different wavelengths, the other within the eye, due to chromatic aberration.

In Cruz-Diez's *Chromosaturations*, rooms are filled with coloured light, but it is not the surfaces onto which colour adheres, instead the light occupies the space as a mist. The early, single-colour projection pieces of James Turrell also display a spatial displacement of colour and light. Rather than sitting on the wall upon which they are projected, each colour appears to inhabit a different plane. While the rectangles of blue light seem to sit in front of the wall, the red light projections recede into the space beyond. It would be wrong to assume that these are nothing more than optical illusions. The brain is making no mistake; the different wavelengths of light are focused at different points inside the eye—the distortion caused by the variation in refractive index of each wavelength of light as it passes through the eye's lens. Blue comes into focus in front of the retina, whereas the focal plane of red lies at a distance behind it. These spatial distortions reveal that light is not fixed in the way that it is perceived. Even before cultural and subjective meaning is taken into account the physical perception of light is in flux.

Dark Matters Inside the eye, impressed on the curved wall of the *retina*, is a map that describes the worlds of light and dark and the transitions between them. Across this map are fields of light-sensitive receptors. At the centre of this map is the *fovea*, a dense accumulation of colour vision receptors oriented towards the *pupil*. These are the *cones*, used for high-acuity vision in bright light. All the colours that we see are constructed by these receptors, attuned to three wavelengths of light: red, green and blue. On the surface of the retina, with the light streaming in through the pupil, the patterns of light excite a matrix of red, green and blue cones to construct an image of a scene outside the eye.

Visible light, as Isaac Newton showed, is made up of a spectrum of different wavelengths ranging from violet to red. Humans do not detect all wavelengths of light directly but see colours when visual receptors are activated to different degrees, in effect mixing the palette of colours of light. The visual experience of white is when all three receptors are stimulated at the same time. What we call white light is often varied in its structure; sometimes constructed from all the wavelengths from violet to red, like daylight or incandescent light, and sometimes with selective wavelengths, like fluorescent strip lighting.

Darkness is defined as the absence of light and by extension

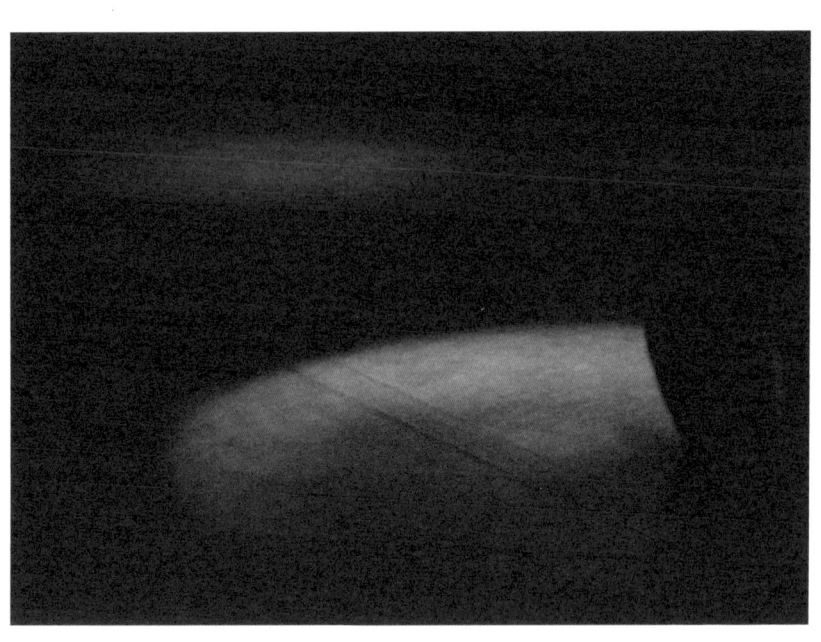

an obstruction of vision. It has a hold on the imagination as the territory of menace; at any moment the person in the dark might come under attack and has no way of knowing where the danger is situated. The brain, starved of information from the eyes, is often filled with fantastic and terrible notions. Although we don't give this superstitious terror much thought, we retain an anxiety about the dark; using light to provide legal protection from accidents that may occur. Specifically, it is not that we know that something will happen but because we don't know where, when or from whom a lawsuit will come.

The dark signals a change to the nature of vision; colour sensitivity shifts toward the blue-green end of the spectrum, bright reds are swiftly extinguished, becoming indistinct from browns and blacks. Covering most of the spherical surface of the retina is a dense accumulation of receptors known as *rods*. Although there are still clusters of colour-sensing receptors outside of the fovea, this territory is the domain of the receptors adapted to low levels of light. This *mesopic* intermediary vision is the threshold before the colour receptors stop working completely and we are plunged into monochromatic night-vision.

In low levels of light a sensory shift occurs as we begin to rely on information coming to our skin. We reach out, strain our ears and become more alert to other sensory cues for information. But before completely handing over responsibility to the other senses, vision itself, in semi-darkness, could be described as becoming tactile so that things out of reach are perceived in a method akin to touch.

There is a material and spatial ambiguity of darkness. Is it a solid? We can't see past it, but we can move through it. Is it a void? It has no discernible surface but seems to have a thickness that is impenetrable even with concentrated focus. Vision, calibrated to detect the edges and boundaries between one thing and another, cannot complete the picture and void becomes indistinguishable from solid. The depth is misleading. Far beyond the reach of the eyes, materials with a high reflectivity pick up minute rays of light and bounce them back.

What matters is what is revealed by darkness, rather than concealed by it. Where it could be understood to be a dense wall blocking vision, the eyes also render a lack of light as a cavity or absence of objects. The dark voids have a structure holding the details and objects that pick up light in place.

In bright light the whole of a scene is identified in a moment. In an instant the eyes have captured an object's shape, texture and its relation to other objects in a room. There is no distinction between which of these details is picked up first, but in darkness, where the information is reduced, details can only be grasped one at a time in a process analogous to touch. With eyes shut and using only the hands, perception of an object is very different; the hands come into contact with it at one place, move across, around and leave at another point. The idea of the object is thus constructed through successive pieces of information. In darkness the eye picks up small pieces of information; a glint of light on a polished surface, the shadow of an outline. The piecing together of visual information in the darkened space allows for a narrative to be constructed with a beginning and an end. It also allows for the possibility of alternative endings and other interpretations, allowing the brain to be creative in completing the picture.

Vision is very efficient at short-cutting that narrative where the light levels are high. This has implications for how we think, imagine or try to be inspired in an everyday setting. Darkness permits the space to think by spacing out the information that we perceive and breaking down the absolute distinctions of things. In bright light, information clamours for our attention. There is no depth of field or hierarchy in an artificially lit office; all points of the room—following lighting codes—are in high-resolution and lit evenly, flattening perception radically.

Cities overflow with light and eclipse the night sky with a luminous fog that exiles total darkness to a concept that exists in the mind; something almost impossible to experience in an urban setting. Inside buildings, shadows are chased out of rooms by banks of fluorescent tubes, saturating the space with an ambiguous unchanging light within which we spend most of the working day. Cut off from the natural patterns of light and dark, these spaces are isolated from external references of time and weather conditions. If a fear of the dark could be said to stem from the sense of disorientation that it causes, it is interesting to note that this condition increasingly occurs in luminous environments.

light

dark

Words for light are not purely literal but have meaning attached. Those to do with light have positive connotations while those associated with darkness are negative. By thinking of words that describe light—or have an etymological relation to it, for example illustrate *from illustrare - to light up, embellish*—and arranging them into two groups, a strong pattern of positive light words and negative dark words can be seen.

The first step in rethinking an approach light would be to somehow destabilise this dichotomy of light and dark. The more dark the word, the more negative its connotation. By giving each word a weighting according to its meaning it could be placed along a scale going from dark to light, with the words *melancholy* and *sombre* being very negative, *dull* and *gloomy* less so, and words such as *shimmer, illuminate* and *brilliant* being increasingly positive.

Why is there such a strong tendency to consider brighter as better, when it is clear that extreme brightness it is not a pleasant experience?

Words like *blinding, flash, dazzle* and *glare* are out of place in a linear arrangement. They are the brightest words and therefore would occupy a position alongside the most positive words. There is also no place for ambiguous words whose value was difficult to determine.

The words value are remapped on the following pages as coordinates along two axes; one for luminosity—its perceived brightness—and the other for value—from negative to positive meaning.

The resulting arrangement reveals an optimum level of brightness before the words drop off into having a very negative association.

By looking at the words across the horizontal direction, an equivalence of meaning can be seen between light and dark words. A *flash* or *blinding* light is an obstruction, as is something *opaque* or *obscure*. To be *dazzled* or to find details *murky* are both expressions of confusion and to *whitewash* something is as deceitful as a *shady* deal.

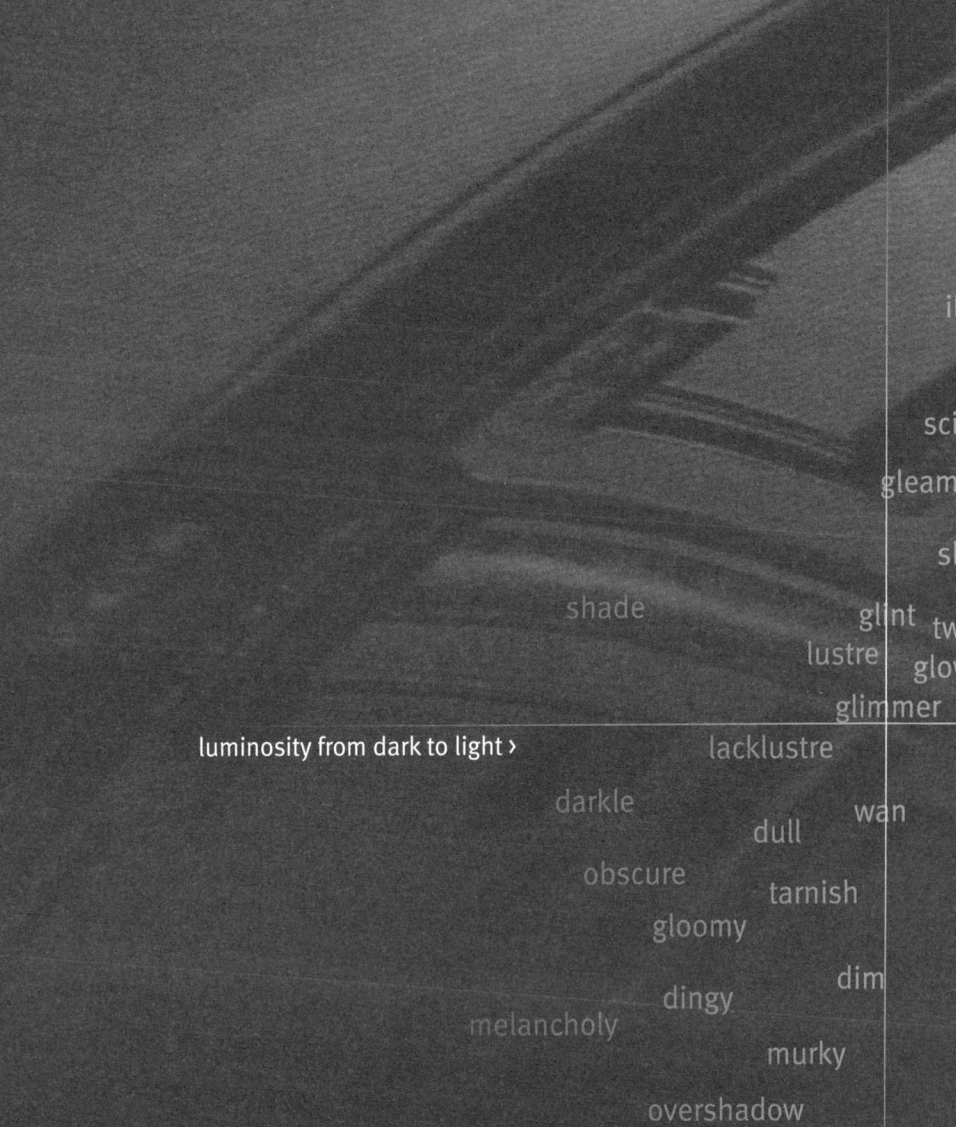

luminosity from dark to light ›

nlighten
us
bright	radiant
highlight	halo
brilliant
beam
shine
illuminate

sparkle

flashback
flare
glare	fulminate
flash
blanch
blinding
blench
flashy
bedazzle
flaw
white-out
whitewash

ow to high

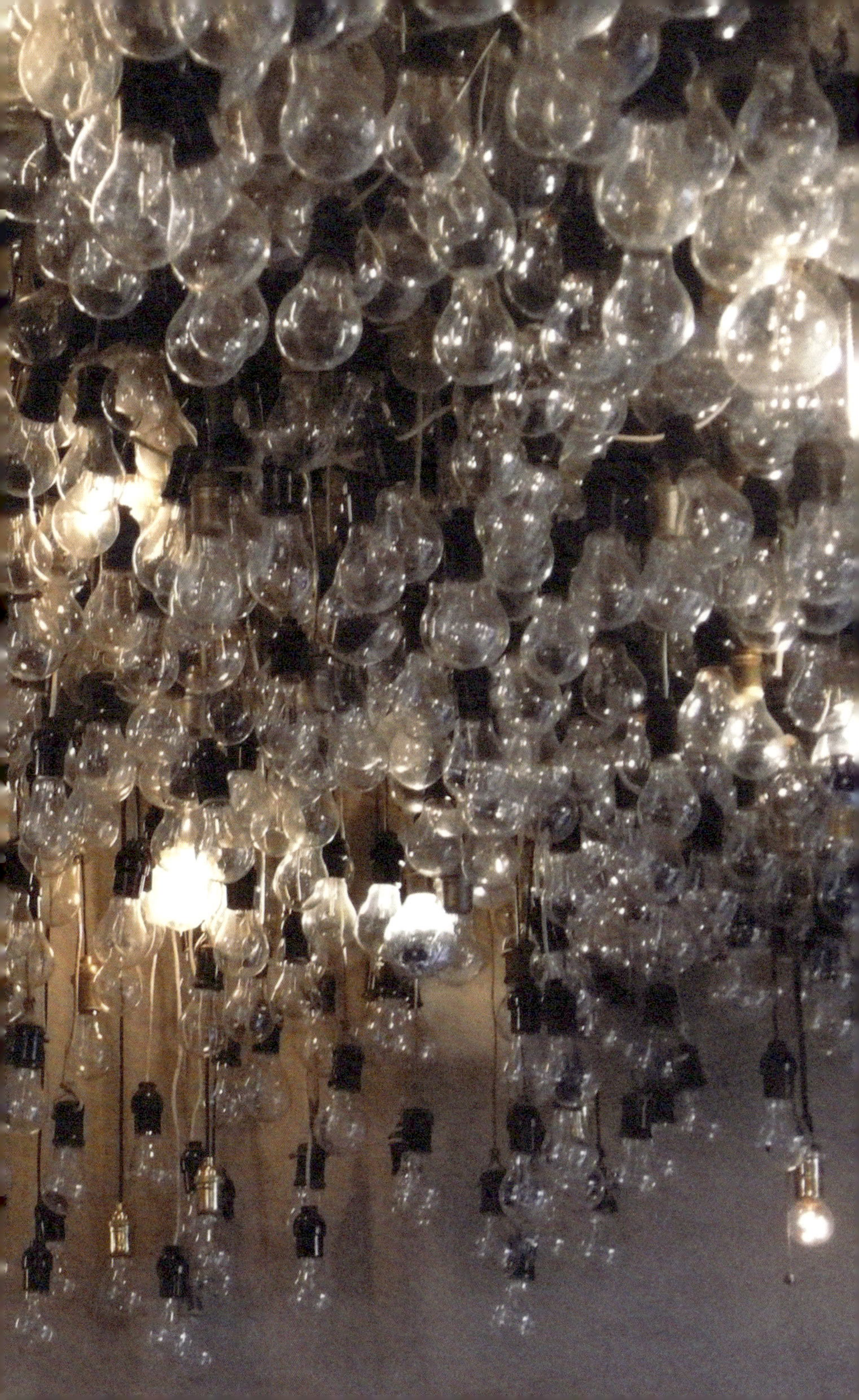

Light Switch
Dark Adaptations

IMPORTANT NOTICE
FROM SEPTEMBER 2009
LIGHTBULBS TO BE PHASED OUT:
ALL PEARL LIGHTBULBS
ALL OPAL CANDLES
ALL OPAL BALL LAMPS
FOR MORE DETAILS
ASK INSIDE

Light Switch The switch substitutes one thing for another—in lighting, on for off and light for dark, suggesting that the two things, through their opposition, are somehow equal. That *on* is not equivalent to *off* becomes apparent when automatic sensors are installed in place of a traditional switch. The feeling of the lights coming on when entering a room, as they are activated by a presence-detecting sensor, is welcoming.

If switching-on could be seen as a benevolent gesture, switching-off is seen as more aggressive; the automatic switch that plunges the immobile worker into darkness is annoying and even mischievous— it is interesting to note that automatic controls, operating independently of human contact, are given anthropogenic characteristics and attributed a certain willfulness.

Even where levels of natural light are sufficient to see by, to switch off the lights in a space where people are working is perceived as a negative interruption. To add light as it begins to get dark is perceived as a thoughtful gesture, although it may not actually be dark yet. Despite there being people who find bright light uncomfortable and for whom switching on an unnecessary light is disruptive, it is nonetheless seen as the right course of action. As if, by sitting in the fading light without noticing, you were making a mistake and needed correcting.

Switching-on, in the sense of lighting a room, is therefore a different problem to switching-off and the switch is more than a device to simply add or subtract light. When a light is switched off, the eye readily adapts to the change in light levels. There remains, however, an after-image; the sense of something having been taken away. This is generally not the case with switching on a light. If we determine that it is not the change in the actual level of light so much as a change of environment that is occurring, it is worthwhile asking—*Who has control of these changes?*

Where once the placement of the light switch by the door

meant that anybody could change the light environment in a room, the controls now reside in another part of the building—generally the services department. In some cases the controls are even physically apart from the building, programmed through software on a portable computer.

Nevertheless, the location of the switch at the threshold to the room has cemented a connection between light and physical presence in a space. To decide for yourself that the room is bright enough without artificial light becomes redundant; you are present and will be lit, or to be more precise, the whole room will be lit for you in a uniform manner anticipating any action or task that you might carry out. The control of light is taken out of the hands of the users and given to the services engineer, who it is assumed knows (objectively) best and can overrule dangerous things such as personal (subjective) opinion and preference.

With the pressing concern of many companies being the environment—an external and global condition—rather than the immediate, interior environment, there is a potential for misuse of lighting controls. Too often what is considered non-functional lighting—usually that which does not light the desk directly—is switched off and a quick and easy saving is made. I make this distinction between functional and non-functional hesitantly, although with a suspicion that such a taxonomy already exists in the installation of lighting in many buildings. By looking at the configuration of the wiring circuit for light fixtures, it is easy to tell which lighting is considered functional in a building.

Typically, lighting layouts are installed before occupation, following a ceiling grid, resulting in light that does not always correspond with what takes place below. Instances where a luminaire has been positioned in a space that is subsequently occupied by a tall filing cabinet are difficult to resolve. Switching off a light where it is not needed requires reprogramming centrally, the rewiring of the loop or the removal of a light fixture, so it is all too often left on. In contrast, accent or decorative lighting, usually on a separate loop, is easy to switch off.

Sensible light planning around the behaviours of the occupants of a building, rather than a strategy based on the programmatic layout of a floor plan, has the potential to be an efficient way to light a space. But it does require the architect and designer to engage with the needs of the people who work there and to deal with real-world (and often contradictory) scenarios.

How is something so fundamentally important to people as lighting treated with such insensitivity? Is it because the understanding of light as a symbol is greater than our understanding of the importance of good illumination?

Abstract concepts such as carbon reduction and energy-saving require a visible or tangible proxy through which to be communicated. It is important that something is seen to be done to demonstrate an awareness and commitment to energy-saving principles. With the notion of electricity signified by the light bulb, the action of switching off the lights becomes a powerful symbol of energy reduction. Meanwhile, in the darkness, devices on stand-by, Wi-Fi, computer servers searching and tweeting continue to draw energy. Power, provided by generators designed to deliver *always-on* energy, moves invisibly around the grid. Furthermore, the switched-off light bulb betrays its embedded energy; the production, shipping and disposal required throughout the product's lifetime.

To be *switched-on*, *geared up* or *plugged in* is to be alert and intelligent. With such mechanic terminology, is it surprising that we look to technology to solve our problems? A problem that is, essentially, the light being left on. In a human context we don't know when or necessarily how to switch off, leaving work with smart technologies that ensure that we are never completely on a break.

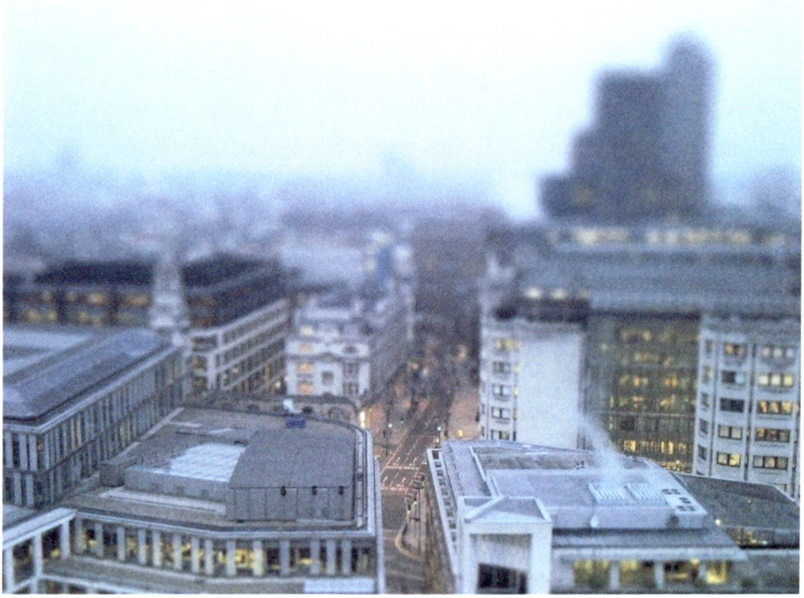

Electric light has changed the way that we live and work, extending the day beyond the threshold of darkness. The human species, whose activities originally took place outside, now spends the majority of time indoors under artificial light. Exposure to the natural daylight under which our species once thrived is greatly reduced.

For those who live in cities, the amount of time spent in natural daylight can be so low that the body seems to inhabit a different time zone. This social jet lag is caused when a person experiences unnatural light environments or social cues about when to be awake, such as night shift work. The human body is directly influenced by bright light, and this is the basis of a science of chronobiology.

In 1962, a French geologist spent two months in a subterranean cave beneath the Alps, cut off from daylight. Sleeping and eating when he felt like it, he discovered the fundamental principle of a theory of human chronobiology; the human body has an internal clock that keeps its own time, synchronising the cycles of hormone release, metabolism and sleep/wake patterns. Bright light, received through the eyes, is the primary influence on this clock, sending a signal to the pineal gland to suppress the release of the sleep hormone, melatonin, during daylight hours. In spaces where there is not sufficient daylight the body experiences a biological twilight and the clock starts to drift out of a 24 hour sequence. When the body receives light at the wrong time, the cycles fall out of step with each other. This desynchronisation of the circadian system exhibits the symptoms of jet lag; disorientation, tiredness, hormone disruption and poor concentration.

The scientific activity and research into the effects of light on the body is now filtering into design and architectural practice. With an understanding of light as an active substance that has properties that affect human biochemistry, the task of lighting a space becomes far more complex than simply illuminating the visual field. This is particularly the case when a further reaction in the body is considered; one that choreographs the acute physiological changes that precipitate alertness, including raised body temperature, heightened release of cortisol (the stress hormone) and an increased heart rate.

To summarise, there are two main influences of bright light on the human body. One is the daily winding of the circadian clock to ensure that we sleep and wake at the right times, the other is an immediate alerting effect. It is this second consequence that is being adopted as an argument for increased levels of light in the workplace; one that is biologically significant enough to promote productivity in the workplace. Light is switching us on.

Dark Adaptations The scientific findings are, so far, being translated directly into pathological expressions; lighting applications that have a specific objective to influence health, wellbeing and alertness. Light, as a result, is being referred to as a *dose* and its properties of intensity and spectral composition are being measured out carefully according to its efficacy in influencing the physiology of the human body.

The scientific information raises intriguing questions about our relationship to light, the status of artificial light in architecture, and the role of the architect or designer. The architect adopts the role of a physician in administering light through the building design to the occupant, who becomes the patient. There are ethical questions. How far should architects and lighting designers be able to manipulate the biology of those who inhabit their buildings? Without the complicity of the occupant these products, in the wrong hands, are a biological hack.

The products that are being developed directly from the data are little more sophisticated than the SAD lamps that became available to treat seasonal affective disorder. A lighting product was recently launched and marketed on its productivity-enhancing qualities. Retailers might make these double-daylight lamps sound as benign as a wholesome breakfast cereal, but there are also side-effects of too much bright light.

A patient of the neuroscientist Professor George Brainard was being treated for severe winter depression with bright light therapy; for two hours a day the patient sat a metre away from a 2500 lux lamp, which is five times the amount of light suggested for a well-lit office. The results were very encouraging; the patient felt happier, more energised and was able to return to work. Following the logic that two hours of light made him feel good, the patient reasoned that with twice as much light exposure, he would feel even better. Indeed, he was charged with energy, fired up, raring to go and it was the middle of winter—a time when usually he could barely get out of bed. He felt great, as people who become hypomanic often do. He only realised that there was a problem when, in the middle of a meeting, he had an urge to climb up onto the conference table and dance to make his point.

It might seem extraordinary that, for a species that evolved in the open air, bright light has the potential to cause such a negative reaction. The modern habitat that we have adapted to does not offer the same conditions as those in nature, and the nature of work has changed too. The physical outdoor labour that took place prior to the industrial revolution has given way to sedentary working practices. So does the logic of bringing high levels of light indoors need to be challenged?

The products currently on the market have been developed in laboratory environments under conditions that specifically rule out any kind of context. Good research data is taken too literally and adapted directly into a product. Architects and designers, rather, operate in a setting where a whole range of factors affect light and the way that it is perceived. It is from their perspective and the messy real-world contradictions they face, that there is a clue why light's influence is not predictable.

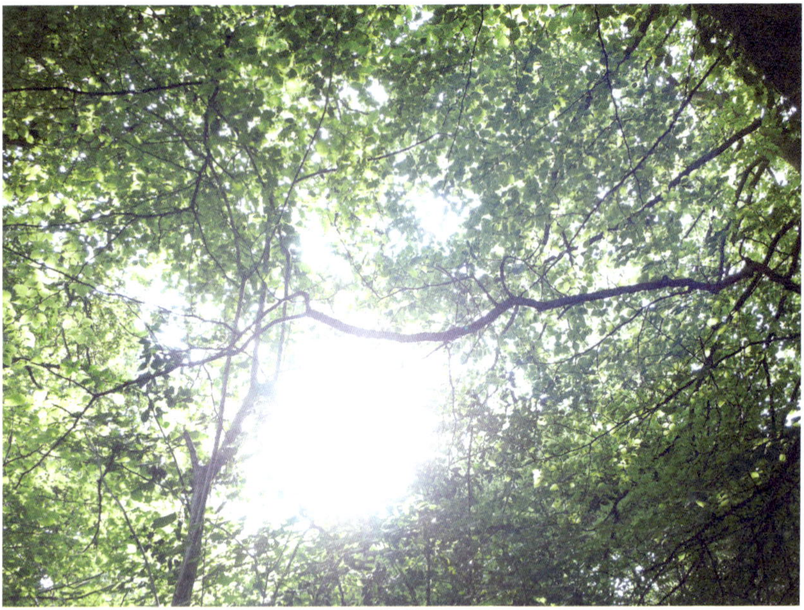

To take the scientific data at face value would be to assume that we live in a milieu of pure light in which there are no surfaces or materials that intercept, reflect, absorb or modify it. These transformations not only influence how we perceive light but also add an important layer of meaning to it. This is more than a symbolic or associative meaning; it is one that illustrates that we are not passive recipients of a light that merely reveals things to be seen. Rather, our species adapted in relation to a specific environment and its luminous characteristics.

In evolutionary terms, the visual and the non-visual systems through which we receive light have not changed since the appearance of the human species. Concentrated in Africa, early hominids—an order of primate to which our own species *homo sapiens* is related—inhabited a continent then covered by vegetation. This provided a verdant habitat, visually foreshortened by the surrounding trees. It might be hard to imagine spatial vision without the concept of linear perspective, but inside a dense forest there is no such thing. Before it was determined and enclosed by straight lines, space would have been understood, visually at least, through stereoscopic vision and light.

In the green light of the forest, space is marked by changes in the luminous field, and the eye is well-adjusted to detect these. The sensitivity of the human visual system peaks at wavelengths of light in the yellow-green part of the spectrum. The colour of sunlight on leaves creates a pattern of bright green and yellow patches in the visual field. These patches of light are determined by gaps in the canopy and clearings. Areas of luminosity, therefore, signify an opening; either an opening-up of space (vertically) or an opening through to another space (horizontally). Instinctively our eyes are drawn to the brightest parts of the scene; they seek out open space.

Artificial light only serves to illuminate those surfaces

that are closed—walls, ceilings and at night, the glazing. The illuminated interior does not follow the same cues as light in the natural environment.

———

As the first of the hominidae climbed down a branch on the taxonomic tree to become a ground-dwelling species, they had to adapt to their changing environment. For our ancestors, to leave the cover of either the forest or a shelter was to be exposed to risk; the stakes were significantly raised as early humans were not only potential prey but predators themselves. Their physiology had to be optimised in order to compete with other species for food. Is it possible that, as they ventured out into open space (and daylight) the biochemical responses to bright light primed them for action? Such an evolutionary benefit to a hunter-gatherer species would be lost on modern man, who spends most of the daylight hours indoors, sitting at a computer.

We modify our environment faster than we evolve, so that the way we live now is vastly different from that of the early human species with whom we share a near-identical biology. Bright light received in the brain has an effect on the whole body, it does not simply activate intelligence. With a distinct possibility that levels of artificial light will increase beyond what we need visually in order to accommodate biologically significant levels, there is a danger that we will be, like Professor Brainard's patient, switched-on with nowhere to go.

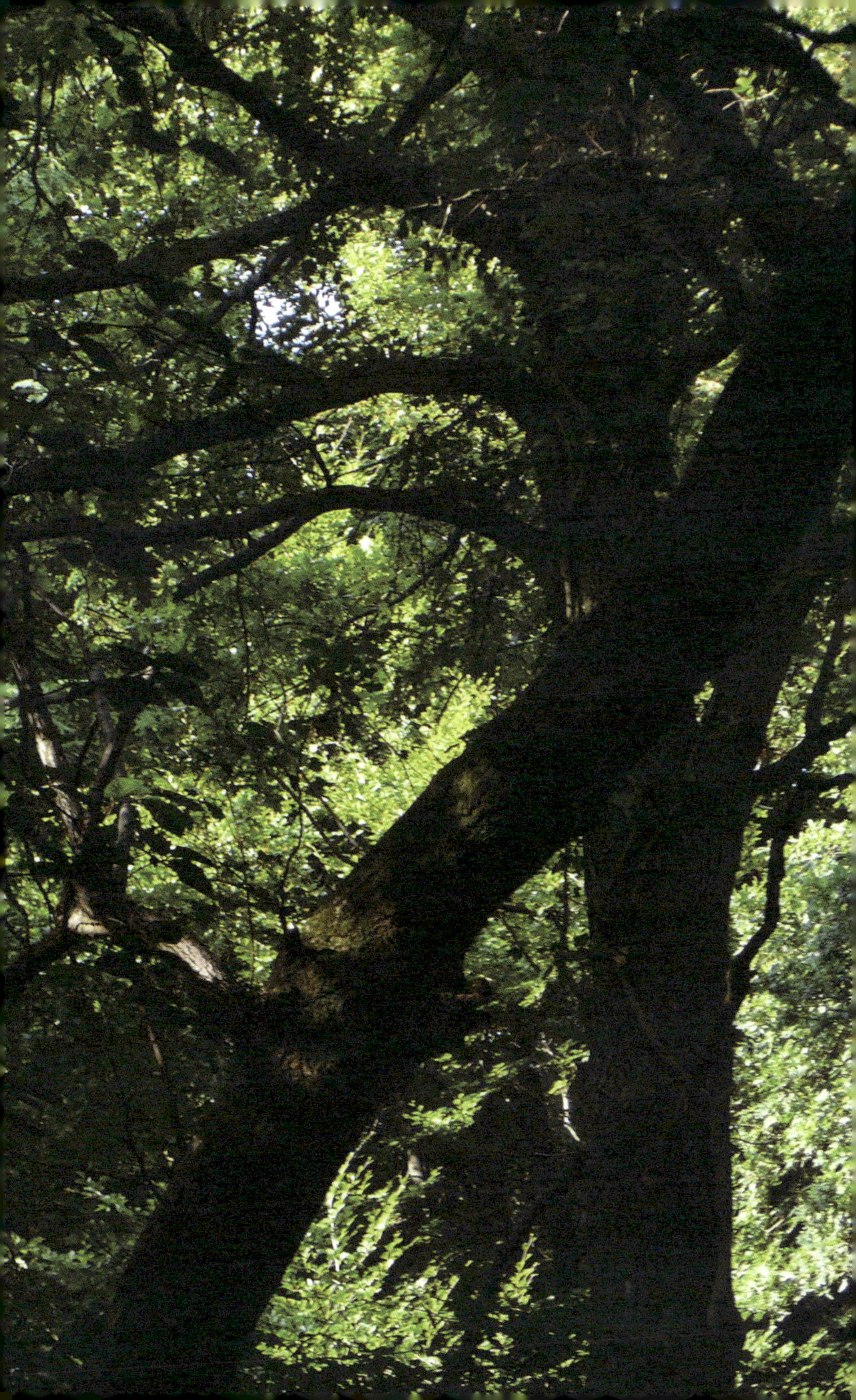

In the dark It is 3.45am in New York and I am free-running in my hotel room, as my body attempts a temporal parkour to catch up to the time zone I have launched it into. I am experiencing first hand the slow drift of the body's internal clock into a sequence of 24 hourly cycles. Yesterday I woke at 3.15am, although I needed more sleep an internal mechanism is overriding this and my waking pattern echoes this sequence.

New York, at street level, is dark even at midday. The rain never stops and the streets, with their skyscrapers at each side, feel like canyons, giving the impression of a buried city where ground level begins at the roof tops. Indeed, my hotel room is suspended twelve floors down the interior wall of an atrium.

I am here to attend Lightfair, but light is hard to find and without it I am predictably contemplating the ceiling of my hotel room at 4.20am the following morning.

Times Square, an area of little over a hundred square metres, contains a complete history of electric light-neon, argon, xenon, incandescent filament bulbs, fluorescent tubes, energy efficient bulbs in primary colours, animated façades encrusted with red, green and blue light emitting diodes. A sudden burst of sunshine seems to hover in the rain-saturated air as a swarm of these tiny lights turn orange.

In this city that never sleeps I am probably not the only person awake. And it is not just the jet lag keeping me up. I had attended a seminar on lighting and health at the conference where a neuroscientist was presenting some of the data on this subject.

As he spoke, the designers, architects and lighting manufactures were faced with an obvious and slightly stinging truth; this scientist knew more than he could impart to his audience in a forty-minute seminar. And the science isn't yet resolved—it is known that bright light has particular effects on the body but there are many problems to work out. He warns us against drawing logical conclusions from the information.

Although we are here to discuss the benefits of bright light, more than anything I think about the problem of too much light: the news that bright light has an effect on a whole range of biological systems, including the nervous system and stress hormones, is particularly problematic. Bright light does not just make you think clearer.

I dream in short bursts about lab mice in darkened shoe-boxes, scrambling around in panic when the lid is removed.

The lighting lab at University College London is a windowless room embedded somewhere deep in the Faculty of Architecture, possibly below ground. It constitutes two rooms; one painted white, the other black. In the black room, the artificial sky—a geodesic frame supporting 270 individually controllable lights—can simulate a number of sky conditions. The white room, where I am being given a crash course in lighting by a tutor from the Masters course, is lit by 36 fluorescent tubes in the ceiling; 24 of which are a special daylight lamp with a colour temperature of 9000 degrees Kelvin. The light level is around 1500 lux. If a normal fluorescent bulb is around 3000K and provides about 500 lux on a desk the amount of light in that room could be estimated to be five-times the amount of a typical office lighting scheme. It was uncomfortably bright, and it was unclear just who was interrogating who.

Later, sitting in the complete darkness of Miroslav Balka's oversized shipping-container sculpture *How It Is* in the Tate Modern, I listen to Hugh Huddy of the Royal National Institute of Blind People, as he talks about his experience of blindness. A man who exists in a field of light—the onset of his blindness was a specular eroding of the darkness—Hugh describes how he always feels *watched*. He is acutely aware that, while he sees nothing, everybody else can see every move he makes. But I wonder if the sensation of being watched contin-uously, is the same for those whose blindness has immersed them in darkness. I wonder if the physiological alertness that is triggered by light is a wariness; some knowledge in the animal brain of being exposed to view.

Der Himmel über Berlin Hovering above the city—although the skies look perfectly clear and blue—is the ash-cloud. Invisible to my eyes, tiny dark particles from the volcano Eyjafjallajökull have brought international sky-travel to a standstill. As the dark matter from the volcano is swept around the earth, I wonder about the effect it will have on sunsets.

Having a few unexpected days to fill, I visit the studio of Olafur Eliasson to speak to Sebastian Behmann about *The Weather Project*, an installation at the Tate Modern. In 2003, Eliasson filled the Turbine Hall with the light from an artificial sun.

Unlike a true sunset, it was possible to walk right up to the back wall to peer behind the sun's surface. The disc was back-lit with an array of mono-frequency yellow lamps creating a light that had nothing to do with full-spectrum sunlight. This light reduced everything seen to monochrome.

The surprising effect of this, Sebastian tells me, is that the eye sees everything in high contrast, despite the loss of colour detail. Mesopic vision—a transitional state between the photopic vision we use in daytime and dark-adapted scotopic vision—allows the eye to see further. The visitors to *The Weather Project* could see themselves reflected in mirrors covering the ceiling at a distance of sixty metres.

The size of the Turbine Hall, notes Sebastian, is almost the same as the Basilica of St. Peter's in Rome. There, a sense of scale and reference to a human scale, comes from its ornamentation. In the Tate Modern, a converted power station, the machine-scale industrial architecture needed a new understanding of size and depth, particularly in order to create a spatial relationship between the visitor and the sun. The space was permeated by an artificial fog, which had the effect of creating a synthetic depth of field, a form of aerial perspective where visitors could judge distance through noting the thickness of the haze.

Against Nature The sun is a point source which, much like an incandescent light bulb, emits its rays outwards from a central point. A common light bulb throws all shadows into perspective projection, but because of the sun's size relative to the Earth, its light rays arrive in a parallel manner.

In order to correctly mimic the light from the sun, but using a point source at a much smaller scale, the light rays have to be refracted so that they are also parallel, recreating the effect of sunlight and the orthogonal shadows that accompany it.

These principles of geometry are important if one is to recreate a rainbow, as engineers at Atelier One were asked to do by the artist Marc Quinn.

If the three elements that determine a rainbow in nature are the light source, the observer and clouds, then those for an artificial rainbow could be the ability to create variability in the size of water droplets, the properties of the light source and the size of the space to contain both a water-tank and an artificial sun. These determine the size of the rainbow and purity of its colours.

In order for the rainbow to work, the light has to be from a direct source and undiffused. It needs to arrive in a parallel orientation to the water in order to form an arc. If the light rays are not parallel, the spectrum loses its arc, and flattens out.

Geometry and scale play an important part in creating artificial light phenomena. Which raises the question— What is artificial light? Is it the artificiality of the means of generating the light or is it that the light itself has no qualities in common with natural light?

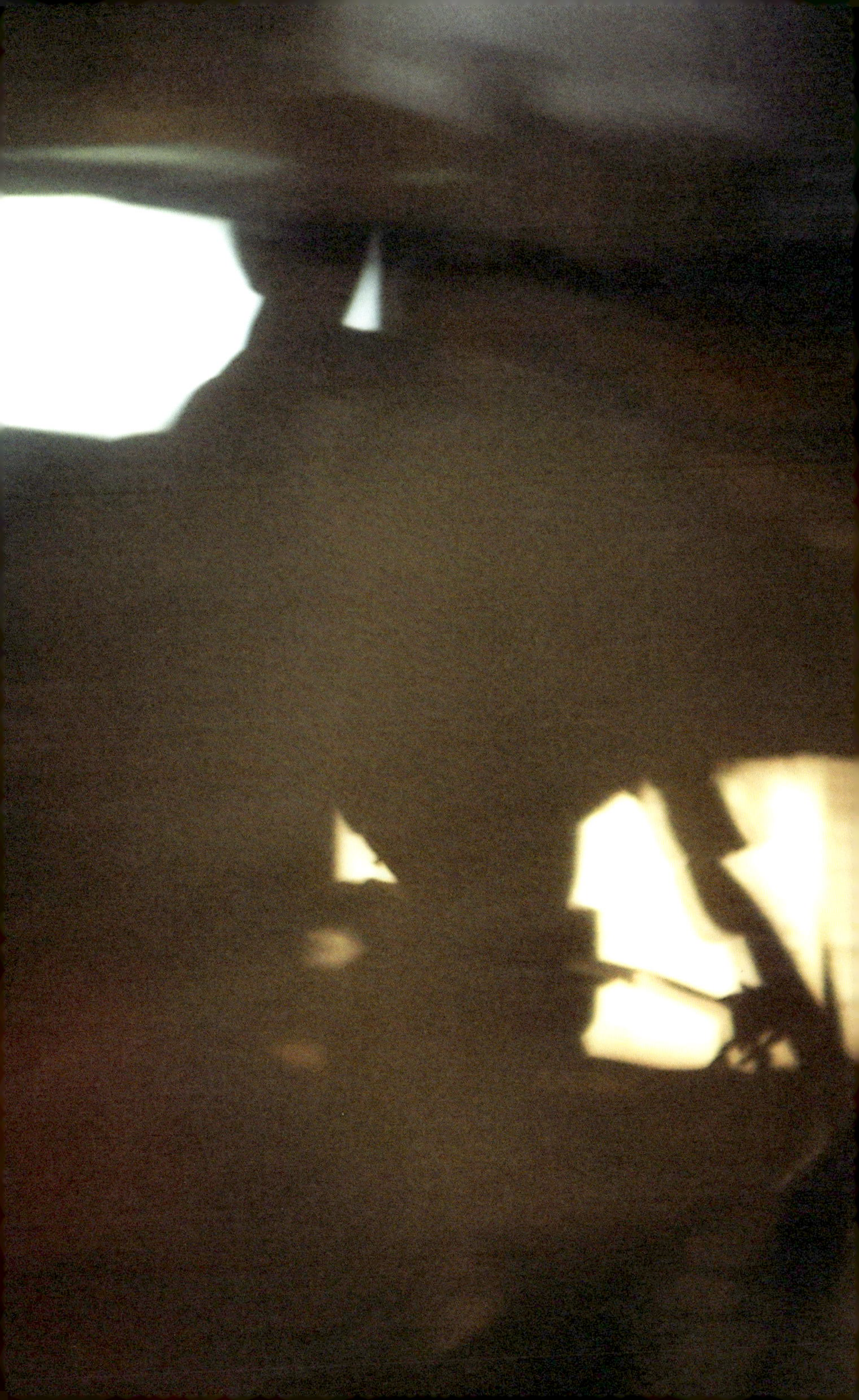

Light Structures
Dark Infrastructure

Light Structures The precise nature of light is undermined at the moment it comes into contact with a person; at this point the variables become apparent. While the amount of light falling on a surface can be measured with a lux meter, its composition of wavelengths determined using a spectrometer, we cannot ever be sure how that light is perceived. Although all eyes follow biological rules, what is perceived by an individual is far more complex. This might suggest that it is too random or complicated and not particularly reliable as an indicator of a good lighting design. But I would like to propose that there are underlying structures to the perception of light.

Throughout the book, the chapters identify at least seven factors in operation within or upon an individual that have the potential to affect how light is evaluated. The definitions that follow attempt to cover the extent of the instability in the relationships between light, space and the individual. *Physiological*—the generic effect of light on all bodies with fully functioning eyes; *biological*—the variations specific to the health and medical circumstances of an individual; *psychological*—including pathological conditions, mental outlook and personal temperament; *cultural*—the associations between luminosity and meaning (including colour); *physical*—the actual properties of light such as illuminance and spectral composition; *environmental*—regarding the weather and climate conditions in a particular geographical location; and *spatial*—the performance of architecture, scale and geometry and the behaviour of light.

These parameters influence each other to varying degrees. Some are subjective and particular to the individual, whereas others affect most people in much the same way. They may be permanent structures that are explicitly present, such as a medical condition. The natural ageing of the eye, for instance, results in a yellowing of the lens that obscures shorter, bluer wavelengths of light. Lupus, the symptoms of which include an acute photosensitivity, completely reconfigures a person's relation to light and their social relations within light. Other factors might be less fixed and relate to a passing mood or particular period of stress that a person is under.

The vast array of possible outcomes presented by these structures would be easier to ignore altogether. Instead of attempting to accommodate every permutation of the perception of light, it is more important to understand that there are also infrastructures that light sits within. These operate at different *speeds* and *scales*.

A methodology could therefore be less about profiling all the different needs of each individual, but more about identifying the different scales that lighting can operate on. In a practical application, a low level of ambient light can satisfy a minimum for the requirement of seeing, as opposed to reading, allowing for a local adaptation of the luminous environment with personal light sources.

A further consideration of spatial configuration allows for more personal variation than simply giving each occupant a task lamp. The objects around each workspace (plants, columns, furniture) are not incidental, but are all potentially active in the way that they reflect, filter, or block light. The surrounding architectural space, the articulation of wall surfaces, the height of the room, the ceiling topography can each be utilised to make more of low levels of light. A space can feel brighter, without using large amounts of light. Lighting designers who are intelligently addressing both user need and energy reduction in their designs have already implemented this volumetric lighting strategy in their offices.

The pace of neurological discovery and technological progress are currently running at altogether different speeds. With medical research needing time to reach certifiable conclusions, it may be upwards of twenty years before we have any definite answers. Indeed, it is likely that there will be even more questions about the human response to light. We are at a stage where it is far too early to draw conclusions; while certain facts have been established—that bright light influences the circadian system in the human body—there are still many unknowns in chronobiology. If the speed of medical discovery is slow, then the work to uncover why the body evolved to respond to light biologically could be even slower. The palaeolithic infrastructure of the body still operates in modern man and researchers are trying to determine exactly the parameters for an intrinsic biological response to specific levels of luminance and spectral composition. Nonetheless these things still have to sit within the wider structures that are personal, cultural and so on. An office in London recently tested an installation of double daylight fittings, but in speaking to the participants after the year-long study, what was revealed was a range of biological, cultural and medical variations that impeded any absolute conclusions.

Meanwhile, the speed of advances in lighting technology has escaped that of a mechanical time scale. The LED industry has shifted the speed of progress to a semiconductor rate of change; the latest innovations in lighting becoming as obsolete as the previous generation of mobile phone. The motivations for lighting are becoming increasingly scientific; architects and designers are now engaging with two key issues on a technological level— sustainability and health. While designers need to know this information, what do they do with all the knowledge from scientific papers? And how do they apprehend these fundamental changes to the spaces in which we live and work, when they happen faster than a thorough critical discussion can take place?

This makes an attempt to write about these problems seem somewhat futile. A book written in the middle of the last century about light is, for the most part, still relevant now. But what can I say now that won't be soon out of date? In the time between these words being typed and being read, the next generation of LEDs will be on the market. Or by the time you finish reading this book, perhaps a new invention will be launched that will make much of what is written about light redundant. But technological progress, if it renews itself so frequently, cannot be the solution to problems of an environmental nature.

Dark Infrastructure While the speed of technological progress increases, the products and solutions—however advanced they are—will have to fit into an existing infrastructure. Inherited from the incandescent age, this infrastructure is slow. It is only those products that interface effectively that will succeed. Thomas Edison may well be remembered for his successful light bulb design, but his legacy is not about to be eradicated with the phasing out of the incandescent lamp. His real innovation was to devise the means of powering light—an electrical power-supply that allowed his product to be ubiquitous.

This point is particularly relevant when trying to negotiate issues of sustainable practice. One of the barriers to sustainability for replacements of the traditional bulb is that they are being shoehorned into an incandescent infrastructure. The latest and most efficient light bulbs come with ballasts and drivers attached to allow them to function with mains electricity. It is necessary to acknowledge that much of the efficiency of new technology is lost through trying to make it compatible with existing electrical fittings. This technology would work more efficiently supported by a suitable low-voltage source.

This signals potentially interesting developments. As we try to upgrade our creaking and inefficient infrastructure; villages in rural India, without mains electricity, are skipping the 20th century completely in terms of lighting, going directly from kerosene lamps to off-grid solar powered LED lighting.

It is a further irony that while we are preoccupied with the symbolic act of substituting one light bulb for another, it is the offspring of other appliances promoted by Edison to exploit his electrical power distribution system that are drawing energy.

Electricity delivered to the home, factory or office could do more than illuminate; it could also power motors and provide heat. A whole species of incandescent appliances—electric toasters, kettles, ovens, hair-dryers and irons—were developed to maximise the benefits of electricity. Motorised devices such as sewing-machines, elevators, and their modern offspring—washing machines, dishwashers and food-processors—all utilised the same technology that brought light indoors. Now there are televisions, games consoles, computers and mobile phones plugging-in to draw power from the system that largely escape scrutiny. As one of my interviewees pointed out—*Why do I have to change my light bulbs, when my neighbour can buy a plasma-screen TV?*

There is a tendency to believe that the solution to the problems of inefficiency and poor quality lie in technological and scientific progress. Inevitably, LED technology will improve, but there is no reference to who is responsible for setting the criteria for improvement—the manufacturer of lighting, the designer or the user? And while there is plenty of solid medical research being conducted, the studies can be very disparate and isolated from each other. It is astonishing that research into the positive effects of blue light on body clock synchronisation has not acknowledged research into the negative impact of blue light on eye health and the link with macular degeneration. At the same time that some researchers are working out how to maximise the efficiency of a light fitting by *boosting* its blue wavelengths, there are others devising coatings for spectacles that cut out these same wavelengths.

Is the attempt to create lab conditions, which rule out any irregularities, hindering the understanding of light for those who design with it? Light, as a physicist might view it, can be described by its properties; electromagnetic radiation with a speed of 186,282 miles per second. It has been diffracted, diffused and perturbed until it is not only a measurable unit but a unit of measurement itself. While the isolation of light's properties tell us much about its microstructure, it doesn't help a designer to illuminate a room well.

Architecture and design is for people, not bodies that respond only to biological stimuli. The negotiation between internal and external forces in each individual, which make up the wealth of lived experience, presents a challenge to the lighting design community.

Instead of trying to get the answer right, architects and designers could come up with the right questions. Indeed the ideas in this book are not the answers but provocations, and are directed as much back to the scientific community as to the user. Design expertise could therefore be carried in both directions, rather than in one—from concept, to product, to the market— in order to address the inadequacies of purely technical solutions.

Bibliography

Bachelard, Gaston The Poetics of Space, Beacon Press 1992

Banham, Reyner The Architecture of the Well Tempered Environment, Chicago University Press 1984

Bazerman, Charles The Languages of Edison's Light, MIT Press 2002

Berger, John About Looking, Bloomsbury Publishing 2009

Bluhm, Andreas Light! The Industrial Age 1750-1900, Carnegie Museum of Art 2000

Boyce, Peter R Human Factors in Lighting, Taylor & Francis 2003

Brandi, Ulrike Lighting Design: Detail Practice, Birkhäuser 2006

Brandi, Ulrike (ed.) The Secret of the Shadow, Light and Shadow in Architecture, Deutsches Architektur Museum 2002

Brandi, Ulrike and Geissmar-Brandi, Christoph Lightbook, The Practice of Lighting Design, Birkhäuser 2001

Calvino, Italo Six Memos for the Next Millennium, Vintage 1996

Casati, Robert Shadows, Unlocking their Secrets from Plato to Our Time, Vintage 2004

Cuttle, Christopher Lighting by Design, Architectural Press 2008

Cruz-Diez, Carlos Reflection on Colour, Fundacion Juan March 2009

Gibson, James J The Ecological Approach to Visual Perception, Psychology Press 1986

Gray, Eileen and Badovici, Jean From Eclecticism to Doubt in Eileen Gray by Caroline Constant, Phaidon Press 2000

Gregory, R L Eye and Brain, the Psychology of Seeing, Littlehampton Book Services Ltd 1977

Hall, Edward T Beyond Culture, Anchor 1989

Ings, Simon The Eye: A Natural History, Bloomsbury Publishing 2008

Lam, William M C Perception and Lighting as Formgivers for Architecture, McGraw-Hill 1977

Mende, Kaoru A Manner in Architectural Lighting Design, Toto 1999

Mende, Kaoru Lighting Design: For Urban Environments and Architecture, Rikuyo-Sha 2006

Minkowski, Eugène Lived Time: Toward a Psychopathology of Lived Space, Northwestern University Press 1970

Minnaert, M The Nature of Light and Colour in the Open Air, Dover Publications 1973

Murray, D VIA: Architecture and Shadow No 11, Rizzoli International Publications 1991

Pallasmaa, Juhani The Eyes of the Skin, John Wiley & Sons 2005

Rasmussen, Steen Eiler Experiencing Architecture, MIT Press 1962

Speirs, Jonathan and Major, Mark Made of Light: The Art of Light and Architecture, Birkhäuser 2005

Tanizaki, Junichiro In Praise of Shadows, Vintage 2001

Index and Notes

adaptation 13, 27, 41, 47, 49, 50, 56, 60

    aerial perspective 56 *The effect of the atmosphere on objects viewed at a distance. The further away the object or landscape, the lower the contrast, the colours are less saturated and shift towards the blue end of the spectrum in the daytime, or red at sunrise and sunset. The effect is due to the scattering of light by particles in the air between the viewer and object being viewed.*

architects 7, 9, 12, 13, 19, 46, 47, 53, 67

architecture 20, 21, 46, 56, 62

    definition of 19 *light, here is not entering the building but illuminating its form as a sculpture. It seems obvious that Le Corbusier is describing a photographic moment rather than an architectural act.*

artificial light 11, 12, 19, 42, 45, 46, 50, 57

    philosophical implications of ~ 19 *"The evening lamp on the family table is also the centre of the world. In fact, lamp-lighted table is a little world in itself and a dreamer-philosopher may well fear lest our indirect lighting cause us to lose the center of the evening room." Gaston Bachelard, The Poetics of Space p171.*

artificial sky 54 *A geodesic frame supporting 270 individually controllable lights that can simulate a number of sky conditions in any geographic location in the world.*

artificial sun 56, 57 *The 'sun' is a halogen light-bulb attached to a silver parabolic dish—travelling along a set of rails it rises, sets and moves across the artificial sky projecting sunlight onto architectural models placed at below. Architects and students use this to get a hands-on experience of the effect of sunlight and shading in their designs.*

automatic controls 13, 41, 42

    as welcoming 41 *In a series of conversations with office workers the automation of lighting introduced the idea that light or lighting controls have an 'intention', to be either welcoming or mischievous.*

biological twilight 45 *term to describe the ambiguous signals of light received through the eye. The body cannot tell whether it is day or night.*

Brainard, Professor George 47 *A neuroscientist at Thomas Jefferson University in Philadelphia, Dr. Brainard has published numerous papers on the effect*

Index and Notes

of light on human physiology and the circadian system over the past 25 years. Speaking at many of the lighting conferences attended throughout this research program, he warns of designers drawing their own logical conclusions from the scientific information presented.

ceiling, 19, 20, 21, 42, 50, 53, 54, 56

as location of light-source 19 *The positioning of a light on the ceiling and directly at the centre, may have little to do with it being an optimum place from which to illuminate a room. Instead it is inherited from the placement of gas-lamps, away from the walls, in order to eliminate the sooting of these surfaces. Above the gas-lamp, a decorative grill vented the sooty waste (the ornamented ceiling rose). Central illumination is still employed in domestic settings, assumed to be a lighting convention, it is instead one based on an obsolete technology.*

~ topography 63 *In the first year of the research project I identified three spatial concepts for interior lighting. 1: topography —the physical articulation, geometry and texture of surfaces. 2: skiagraphy—the articulation and meaning of shading and shadows in a room. 3 choreography—the change of colour temperature and intensity of light over the course of a day.*

chronobiology 45 *from Chronos—from the ancient Greek word for time. The field of biology that examines the cyclic mechanisms of biological activity in organic life.*

and unknowns 64 *"Even biologists are asking what it means" Professor George Brainard.*

circadian system 45, 64 *from circa (around) – dia (day) describes the approximately 24 hour cycles of biological, physiological and behavioural systems in humans, animals, plants and bacteria. There is an excellent chapter describing the circadian system in Peter Boyce's book Human Factors in Lighting.*

computer screen 23, 24

Cruz-Diez, Carlos 24 *photos pp14-15, 54, 55 © the author, Chromosaturations at Museu Fundación Juan March, Palma de Mallorca.*

darkling 35 *Adverb 1. in the dark. Adjective 2. growing dark 3. being or occurring in the dark; dark; obscure 4. vaguely threatening or menacing.*

dark infrastructure 65 *In the 1980's a system of fibre-optic cable was installed*

Index and Notes

 underneath London for the nascent information industry. This unused infrasctructure was called 'dark-fibre'.

darkness 12, 27, 28, 29, 33, 41, 43, 45, 54
 structure of ~ 28 *Eugène Minkowski describes the spatial nature of light and dark space. In light, he says, we see not only the objects but the spaces in between the objects. There is a presence of 'space' in empty space. Dark space, he asserts, in contrast to light space has no 'beside', but does have an inherent spatial nature which he calls depth. Minkowski, Lived Time pp427-433.*
 ~ **and imagination** 27, 28 *Juhani Pallasmaa believes that the realm of dim light and shadow are catalysts for imagination. "In order to think clearly, the sharpness of vision has to be suppressed, for thoughts travel with an absent minded and unfocused gaze. Homogenous bright light paralyses the imagination" Pallasmaa, The Eyes of the Skin p46.*
 ~ **and narrative** 28 *Idea inspired by a passage in the novel, Lord Jim "He lit a two-branched candlestick and led the way. We passed through empty dark rooms, escorted by gleams from the lights Stein carried. They glided along the waxed floors, sweeping here and there over the polished surface of the table, leaped upon a fragmentary curve of a piece of furniture, or flashed perpendicularly in and out of distant mirrors, while the forms of two men and the flicker of two flames could be seen for a moment stealing silently across the depths of a crystalline void." Joseph Conrad, Lord Jim pp164-165.*

daylight 25, 45, 47, 50, 54, 64

double-daylight 47, 64 *A term used to describe an artificial light source with extra blue wavelengths. Blue wavelengths are present in large amounts in natural daylight. By boosting the amount of blue in a fluorescent light source, it is intended that a short exposure to this light will have a similar effect to spending several hours spent in natural light.*

Edison, Thomas 65, 66

Eliasson, Olafur 56

environment 7, 9, 11, 12, 19, 21, 29, 41, 42, 45, 47, 49, 50, 62, 63, 65

evolution 13, 49, 50

Eyjafjallajökull 56 *The Icelandic volcano that erupted during Light + Building*

Index and Notes

Conference in 2010, stranding many of the 180.000 trade attendees and their light bulbs in Frankfurt. After the 1883 eruption of Krakatoa, small particles in the atmosphere diffracting the rays of the setting sun were said to be responsible for altering the colour of the evening sky, and to have inspired the vivid sunsets in the paintings of Edvard Munch, Joseph Turner and Caspar David Friedrich.

the eye 11, 12, 19, 24, 25, 27, 28, 41, 45, 49, 56, 62, 66

    ageing eye 62 *The lens of the eye thickens and yellows over age. This yellowing cuts out the transmission of blue wavelengths into the eye due to spectral opponency.*

    architectural eyes 20, 21

    chromatic aberration of the ~ 24 *A type of distortion, where the lens does not focus all wavelengths to the same point. Short wavelengths are refracted more than long wavelengths meaning that the focal point of blue and red are different.*

    ~ **and light-dark adaptation** 27, 41, 56

fear of the dark 27, 29

    ~**and disorientation** 29

    ~**and legal consequences** 27 *Identified by Lighting Designer, Edward Bartholomew in his essay on darkness. "As I gaze upon over-lit lobbies and malls, I sense that what is being lit is not the space but merely a fear—legal or otherwise—of the consequence of darkness." Bartholomew, A Place for Darkness pp38-41 in Professional Lighting Design magazine, Sep/Oct 2004.*

Gray, Eileen *see* shutters

homo sapiens 49

light 11, 19, 23, 24, 25, 66

    correctness of ~ 41 *One of the interviewees identified a morality about whether one switches on the lights when they arrive at work in the morning. He felt that his colleagues viewed him with suspicion if he was sitting at his desk without the lights on. "When I get into work in the mornings, I often leave the strip lighting off, and then someone comes in, there is almost a moral confusion that anyone would walk into a room and not turn the lights on as if you'd be doing something somehow wrong. As if it's*

Index and Notes

compulsory, like turning on the printer."
diffused light 23, 24
    dose of ~ 46
    ~ and productivity 11, 46
    religious light 23 *"Catholic light comes from above, Buddhist light comes from the side and Islamic light sparkles from many points" - Oscar Peña, Senior Creative Director at Philips Design.*
    ~ as a symbol 43, 49, 65
lightness 23 *The concept of lightness is one of Italo Calvino's Six Memo's for the Next Millennium.*
light source 19, 56, 57, 63
    ~ **observer and clouds** 57 *from interview with Neil Thomas, director of Atelier One*
light therapy 47 *story told by Professor George Brainard at Light + Building, Frankfurt 2010.*
luminosity 23, 24, 33, 49, 62 *for an excellent article on the social, spatial and metaphorical role of luminosity see An Anthropology of Luminosity a paper by Mikkel Bille and Tim Flohr Sørensen.*
Lupton, Martin *see* volumetric lighting
Minkowski, Eugène *see* darkness, structure of ~
Newton, Isaac 25
Pallasmaa, Juhani *see* darkness, ~ and imagination
parkour 53 *(also known as free-running) A physical discipline practiced in urban environments where a participant travels from A to B using only the body to negotiate obstacles in the way, usually by vaulting, climbing and leaping.*
pineal gland 45 *A gland in the brain which produces the hormone melatonin, which regulates sleep/wake cycles. Long before its functions were understood, the philosopher and mathematician, René Descartes wrote much about this gland, believing it to be the seat of the soul and the point where mind and body met. He wrote "I cannot find any part of the brain, except this, which is not double. Since we see only one thing with two eyes, and hear only one voice with two ears, and in short have never more than one thought at a time, it must necessarily be the case that the impressions*

Index and Notes

which enter by the two eyes or by the two ears, and so on, unite with each other in some part of the body before being considered by the soul." correspondence dated 29 January 1640, cited in Stanford Encyclopedia of Philosophy.

rainbow 24, 57

reflectivity 28 "Above the catacombs of beetles wooden tablets were hung at irregular intervals. The light reached one of them, and the word Coleoptera written in gold letters glittered mysteriously upon a vast dimness."—Joseph Conrad, Lord Jim p156.

refraction 19, 24, 25, 57

seasonal affective disorder (SAD) 46 also known as winter depression, first described by Dr. Norman E. Rosenthal in the 1984 after studying the effects of light on patients suffering from depression with seasonal changes.

shutters 20, 21 "Windows without shutters are like eyes without eyelids"— Eileen Gray, From Eclecticism to Doubt, 1929. Although she was referring to the ventilation problems with windows, this statement encouraged me to view windows as anatomical features and dissect them as such.

Siffre, Michel 45 The geologist spent 63 days in a subterranean cave living "like an animal, without a watch, in the dark, without knowing the time." His discoveries that the body has an internal clock that runs on $24^{1}/2$ hourly cycles has led to light being identified as the most important influence on the body clock. In 1999, he returned underground for 60 days to study the effects of ageing on the circadian system and rung in the new millennium with champagne and foie gras—three and a half days late.

social jet lag 45 Identified as the desynchronisation of the body clock due to social cues, or lighting at the wrong time of the day in cities.

spectral composition 46, 62, 64

synchronisation 45, 66 The eye directs non-visual light information to the suprachiasmatic nucleus; a small part of the brain that acts as the clock-watcher, keeping track of internal biological time and external patterns of light and dark. Each day it takes cues from daylight to 'wind' the clock.

switch 12, 41, 42, 43

Times Square (New York) 53

Index and Notes

Turrell, James 24 *"If you put [coloured light] on a wall it doesn't seem to reside on the same plane as the wall, red and blue colours reside on different planes."—James Turrell, opening speech at Lightfair, 2009.*

vision 11, 21, 24, 25, 27, 28, 33, 49, 50

volumetric lighting 63 *A strategy being implemented by Building Design Partnership "The ambient light was designed to about 200 lux, with task lighting. That worked on the floors where the ceilings were high and there was a lot of space; we were able to bounce the light off the architecture and create a perception of brightness. Where the ceiling was a bit lower, we started with that strategy, but there wasn't as much of an opportunity to create volumetric and spatial lighting. In response to the user's feedback we raised the ambient lighting level to about 400, still lower there than most offices you would walk into."—Martin Lupton, chair BDP.*

window 12, 20, 21 *Literal translation, wind-eye, the term window comes from Old Norse vindauga from vindr "wind" + auga "eye".*

    anatomy of a ~ 20, 21 *"The well-designed Georgian window was carried up to near ceiling level, allowing light to penetrate to the back of the rooms. Architects were well aware that sharp contrasts between the intensity of the light source and the interior dark areas caused discomfort to the room occupants; they therefore splayed the inside reveals in order to soften the light and overcome the sudden transition from window to dark surrounding wall. It was also a practice to paint the outside brick reveals white or cream up to the window frame to reflect light into the room. These details of construction showed intelligent appreciation of window requirements and, as an example of technique, are not surpassed even today when glass walls can sometimes prove to be too much of a good thing."— F. Palmer Cook, Talk to Me of Windows pp52-53.*

    light from a virtual ~ 24 *For a critical account of light through technology see the chapter Light Time, Paul Virilio, A Landscape of Events pp44-52.*

About the Author

Claudia Dutson started out her career in media in the 1990s when analogue methods of production were rapidly being made redundant by the arrival of digital technology. The emergence of a new digital paradigm presented opportunities for both media and design. Claudia worked in media consultancy for three years, co-writing reports on the convergence of new technologies and developments in digital media.

As Enron's collapse reconfigured the new media industry, Claudia had already been redirecting her career. She started a degree in Architecture at the University of East London, where the question of digital vs. analogue was further addressed. Her research expanded to challenge other dichotomies in architecture such as culture/nature, theory/practice and the predominance of visual experience over a tactile one, particularly with reference to design processes.

After graduating from the Royal College of Art with an MA in Architecture in 2008, she worked as a research associate at the RCA's Helen Hamlyn Centre until 2010.

Acknowledgements

I am grateful to all those who participated in the research for their time and insights, and the support of Sharon Pang, Eddie Smith, Fred Bass and Sean O'Callaghan.

Thank you to:

Martin Lupton, Mark Ridler, Sharon Stammers, Bob Venning, Arfon Davies, Vasiliki Malakasi, Oscar Peña, Chris Jackson, Edward Bartholomew, Ilse Crawford, Jane Withers, Nigel Coates, Fernando Rihl, Hilary French, Gareth Williams, Clare Johnston, Jeff Willis, Ian Whittaker, Jo-Anne Bichard, Catherine Greene, Lez Ingham, Victor Buchli, Ben Allen, Hugh Huddy, David Yost, Michael Chadwick, Jake Moulson, students of Architecture at the University of East London and the University of Brighton.